Table of Contents

Introduction
1: The Early Years
2: New Home
3: Danny
4: Starting Over
5: Hidden Treasure
6: Transition
7: The Real World
8: Planning The Future
9: The Proposal

Introduction

New Years Eve 1983, Tom walked into a bar after a hard day of work. He sat at the counter and told the bartender to make it a double. While sitting there, he thinks about his life,

"I had a good childhood, great parents, with great jobs. I was ok in school, where did I go wrong?" said Tom to the barender, "I guess I could've did better in school, maybe went to college but for what? The only thing I was ever good at was partying".

As he drank time went by, it was a

new year and the bar was the last place he should've been. At this time he was very drunk but so was everyone else. It was New Year's Day so nobody paid him no mind.

"I just wish I knew where my mom and dad were. I wish they had a chance to get to know Jenny and the baby. My girl is at home pregnant with my son. My parents will never know their grandson all because of me", he turned and said to the fellow next to him.

"Thats nice", said the fellow sarcastically.

Feeling disrespected, Tom broke a beer bottle over the man's head. Unfortunately for Tom there was an off duty police office in the bar. As the guy laid on the floor bleeding,

Tom was carried out in handcuffs.

A few days later, Tom was able to have his lawyer contact Jenny, to inform her that Tom was going to be in jail for a few months for assault. Jenny now eight months pregnant went into early labor due to stress after hearing the news.

Chapter 1
The Early Years

James Peterson was born January 6, 1984, since he was premature it was about a week until they were able to leave the hospital. Once they got home it was just the two of them and Jenny was a little scared. Jenny didn't have any family around to help and she didn't really know anyone in the neighborhood except the lady next door. The only good thing about their situation was the money Jenny had been saving from before she stopped working and

Tom went to jail. She figured it would last them for a couple of months. James was a good baby, he didn't cry too much. They had their own routine, starting with a bath and breakfast in the morning, ending with stories at night and all the talking in between. James might not have understood her at first but her voice relaxed him. James and his mother had a good four months of bonding before Tom got out of jail.

Tom was so happy to be with his family and hold his son. Jenny talked to Tom about James on the phone but for Tom it wasn't the same as holding him in his arms. Tom promised them that he would never get in trouble or leave them again. Jenny couldn't stay mad at Tom for long. She was just happy to have some help. It took Tom about two weeks to find a job. He worked hard everyday to make sure the double J's(James & Jenny) had everything they needed. As James grew up, he knew he was loved by both his parents. When birthdays and Christmas came around his parents may not have had much but they did their best to give James everything he needed. James was a fast learner. By the age of two he could go to the bathroom by himself, say his alphabets, his full name and count to 20. The next year he was off to preschool. Jenny didn't want to be away from him because he was still small, so she volunteered at his school for the first two years. When James started the first grade Jenny went back to work to help out financally, but mostly so she could start planning her and Tom's wedding. Jenny made time to take

James to and from school everyday which gave them more time to talk. James's mother explain to him why his father wasn't in his life when he was born and why he had never met his grandparents. James somewhat understood why his father's parents thought he was a trouble maker. He didn't understand why his mother's family stopped talking to her because she stayed with Tom. Jenny promise her son that would never happen to him. James took comfort in knowing that his parents would always love him no matter who he wanted to be with.

Six month later James's parents went to go to the court house and got married. Jenny was so happy when she came to pick James up from Sally's(the lady next door) house after the ceremony. She was so excited to finally be Mrs. Harrison. Tom and Jenny only wished that James was well enough to had been there to experience it with them. Jenny was really looking forward to their lives together. For James nothing really changed. He still had the happy home with two parents that loved him. His mother still took him to school and picked him up. He saw his father every night for dinner and on his dad's days off they watched TV together. The bond between his parents was strong in his eyes, but what did he know, he was just a kid. Tom and Jenny couldn't believe two years had passed without them noticing it or changing James name from Peterson to Harrison.

James always anticipated spending quality time with his

mother after school. One day when James was in the third grade, he waited an hour after school to be picked up. To his surprise, it was his father rather than his mother as usual.

When James asked "Where's mommy?" his father never responded.

Once they got home, Tom sat James down and told him that his mother had got hit by a car. After letting out a long sigh Tom continued,

"the doctor couldn't stop the bleeding and your mother is not coming home.

James didn't understand, with a puzzled look he asked "how long will she be in the hospital?"

It was so hard for Tom to explain

death to a seven year old, trying to stay strong Tom murmured that she wasn't. It took James a little time to fully understand death, he just knew his mother wasn't there. For James his mother was everything, his world was turned up side down. Tom tried to make things easier for James. He moved his work schedule around so he could take him to and from school. He even told him stories at night and helped him with his homework. Tom tried to tell James why he hadn't talked to his parents in ten years but he couldn't remember. The last thing he heard, they moved down south three years before James was born.

Over time, Tom and Sally had became close. Which came in handy when Tom worked late, on the weekend or wasn't feeling well and needed rest. Sally and James had fun together once he got to know her. They did arts and crafts, ate snacks, play board games, watched TV and Sally told him stories. Most of them were about her kids, how they were grown and how she wanted James to meet them someday. One Saturday evening James and Sally had so much fun, they didn't notice that Tom didn't pick James up after work. Sally thought nothing of it. She assume he must had been tired and went home to bed again.

"I'll take you home in the morning", Sally told James.
Before she had the chance, there was a knock at the door.

"How can I help you?" asked Sally.

"Sorry to bother you, but my name is Robert and I work with Tom

Harrison. There was an incident at work and Tom wanted me to get in contact with you", replied Robert.

"Oh my goodness, is Tom alright?" asked Sally.

"He had a bad cough at work today. Then he started coughing up blood, so a coworker took him to the hospital. He didn't have your phone number on him but Tom gave me your address. Tom just want to make sure you knew what was going on and was ok with the boy", said Robert.

"Oh yes, we'll be fine. He just might need some clothes for school on Monday", replied Sally.

"I'll see what I can do, I'll be in touch", said Robert.

After he left Sally took a moment before she called James in to tell him what happened. By the look on his face she knew he had over heard.

"How much did you hear?" Sally asked.

"My dad is in the hospital", replied James, "is he gonna die too?"

"I don't want you to think like that, I'm sure we will see him soon", said Sally as she rubbed his back.

Five hours later Robert returned with the keys and the direct number to call to check on Tom's condition.
"If he trust you with his son then I guess he can trust you with his keys. When you do call the hospital I don't know how much information they

will give you. I had to say I was family to get the keys", said Robert.

Sally and James went next door to get some of James's school clothes, which made him more sad. Sally waited a day or two before she called to check on Tom. But when she did there was good news. Tom was feeling little better and wanted to see James. After school Sally took James to see his father. They were so happy to see each other. James talked about school and time at Sally's house, but they didn't mention how sick Tom was at first.

Meanwhile, Sally was in the hall talking to the doctors about Tom's health.

"Tom gave me permission to talk to you about his condition. From talking to him, we've gather that he's been sick for a while. We have to run some more test before we know what's wrong. He's stable now, we will know more once we get the test results", the doctor explained.

Sally went back in the room with James and his father. While there Tom told James they were still running test and he didn't want him to worry. Later Sally took James back to her house, silence filled the car as they drove. James went to school for the next couple of days but he really didn't seem focused or like himself.

A week later while James was in school, Tom's doctor called to tell Sally that she needed to come to the hospital. When she arrived he introduced her to the pulmonologist. The specialist informed her that after doing a biospy, Tom has stage four lung cancer and because it has lingered, his condition is worst.

"We had to act fast with his treatment as well as thinking about the future for his son. There's a social worker and Tom's lawyer waiting for you in Tom's room", explained the pulmonologist.
Sally walked into the room, chills ran through her body as she saw that Tom was now on oxygen and couldn't talk much.

"Hello my name is Mary, I'm the social worker on Tom's case and this is Mr. Thomas, Tom's lawyer. We have a lot to talk about, please have a seat. As you know Tom's condition has gotten worst and Tom wanted you to keep James if anything happens to him. However after doing a backgroung check, I see that you are unable to adopt him", said Mary.

"We have filed paper work for you to be James's temporary guardian if that's ok with you. The only catch is that when Tom pass away James will have to go into foster care within the week", explained Mr. Thomas.

"Ok, what about James's schooling? How long do the doctors think Tom has?" asked Sally.

"The doctors are giving him a week or two but if they can keep the fliud off his lungs it might be longer", answered Mary, "and James would have to transfer from his school to the one at the orphanage".

Sally took sometime and let

everything sink in. She really didn't know how to feel or what to think. Sally just knew she had to be there for Tom and James.

"Where do I sign and do you know where James will be placed?" Sally asked.

"No not right now but there's a couple of place I will check out once I leave here", said Mary.

Mary, Mr. Thomas and Sally talked a little more to iron out all of the details before Sally thanked Tom for trusting in her and went to pick up James from school. Sally had mixed feelings about everything. She was devastated about Tom's condition. At the same time was scared of having the responsibility of an other person. She loved James like he was own but taking care of him full time was a big step. Sally just hope that she would do a good job. She knew that Tom death would just destroy James. As she drove she tried to figure out how she would tell James the news. After she explained everything to him, James wanted to go see his father. Sally promised him they would go see him the next day.

James took two steps, turned around and asked "why can't I stay with you, you can just adopt me right?"

"Oh James I wish I could but I'm not finacially or physically qualified to be a foster parent. Which makes me unable to adopted you", replied Sally, "I hope you understand".

"Yes, kind of, not really, but you

would if you could right?" asked James.

"I'm sorry it's kind of hard to explain, but yes in a heartbeat", said Sally, "but I'll come to visit you as much as I can".

The rest of the day James was very quiet. He said he was thinking. When morning came James was up at six ready to go see his father. Sally had to make him eat something while telling him that visiting hours didn't start until ten. When they finally got there James gave his father a big hug and told him he loved him. Tom tried to explain to James a little more about the orphanage, when he was able to take the oxygen mask off.

"When you go to the orphanage you have to be good boy. The school is on the same property as the orphanage so you won't have to walk far", explained Tom.

James listened like he never listened before, then said, "I'm just glad I could be here with you now. I just wish I could stay with you all the time".

"I'm sure he feels the same, but you have to go to school, so you can make your mother and father proud", said Sally.

They talked a little more, then Tom asked James to wait in the hall while he spoke to Sally. James left the room but not before he gave his father one last hug. When James left the room Tom gave Sally a letter.
In the letter Tom thanked Sally for all she had done. The letter stated

he'd made all his arrangements for his funeral and to have his things donated to charity after he's gone. It said he would liked it if she went to the house first and take anything she may liked. The letter ended with Tom asking if she could make sure James packed all his things and that he got something to remind him of his mother and him.

"Normally I would say that's not necessary but I know how you are and it being your last wish I won't argue with you", Sally said to Tom after reading the letter.

After James and Sally left the hospital Sally did exactly what Tom asked of her. She helped James get all his things packed, gave him some family photos and picked out some things for herself. The next week she went to James's school to explain the situation and let them know that she was going to be James's temporary guardian for the rest of his time at the school. The school was sorry to hear about Tom's health and sad to hear that James wouldn't be at the school much longer.

As time passed James wanted to see his father everyday, but in the letter Tom asked Sally not to bring him back. He didn't want James to see him die. May 20, 1992, about a week after their last visit to the hospital and almost one year after Jenny died, Tom passed away. James was mad at the world.

"Your father made me promise not to bring you back to the hospital. He wanted you to remember the good times. He didn't want you to see him die, I'm sorry", Sally explained trying to console James.

James didn't speak, barely ate and

cried himself to sleep every night until the funeral and days after. Sally didn't know what to do. She made him a photo album with the photos they got from the house and told him as long as he kept his parents in his heart they would never be gone.

    By the next week everyone saw a real difference in James but it was understandable. Because of Tom's quick death, Mary wasn't able to get James into an orphanage. James got to finish the school year with Sally. Sally didn't know how James was going to be without school to keep him occupied. When his mother passed he had his father to get him through it. She thought she was doing the best she could but Sally was worried he would act out at the orphanage. Sally and Mary tried to keep James thinking positive about the orphanage, but no matter how hard they tried he still wasn't happy that he was going. James told them he didn't want to leave his friends or school.

A week after school ended, Mary contacted Sally to inform her that James would be going into foster care the next day. After Sally hung up the phone she sat for a minute, not know how she would tell James.

"James, can you come here for a minute?" Sally said, "Sit down I have something I need to tell you".

"How long do I have before I have to leave?" James asked.

"Mary will be here to pick you up tomorrow at noon. I know it's kind of soon but I'm just a mile away. I'll come see you as often as I can", Sally replied.

They both sat quiet for a while before James got up and went in the room to pack. James stayed in the room for the rest of day. He didn't even eat dinner.

Charter 2
New Home

The next day came and it was time for James to go to the orphanage. Sally told James if he didn't cry neither would she.

"We're not saying goodbye, just see you later", said Sally, "you may not live with me but you are always welcome here. I'll be seeing you soon".

James said goodbye to Sally and thanked her for everything, then got in the car with Mary, to go to the orphanage. James was really quiet on the way there. When they walked into the orphanage everyone was in the "meeting room" as they call it. All eyes were on James as everyone waited to meet their new house mate.

"I would like everyone to meet James Peterson. He will be staying with us for a while. I would like everyone to help him fit in and get to know the place", said Sharon the head lady at McMichaelson Orphanage and Learning Center.

"A little while yea right, that's what they told me almost three years ago", whispered Danny in the corner.

James heard him and snicked. Danny was the only person James talked to when he did talk. James didn't participate in class. He did his school work in the corner by himself and he never did any school activities. For the first couple of months James didn't even talk to staff. When he finally did, it was only after Sally visited. He only said he missed his mom and dad. Sally told him she would try to visit him every three months but he had to show some improvements.

"I can't imagine how hard this is for you but can you at least try for me", said Sally, "remember you didn't like me at first but see how much fun we have together now".

"That was different", said James.

"I know, but part of growing up is learning how to cope in different situations", added Sally.

"I'm only 8, I don't wanna be in these situations", James shouted in an angry tone.

"I know sweetie, I'm sorry, I know it will take you sometime and I shouldn't have tried to rush you", said Sally.

Days later one of James class mates asked if he was going to help with the group assignment. Within seconds James yelled,

"No, I'm not doing anything. Where have you been, do I ever do anything with y'all stupid ass kids".
Then he ran out the classroom. It took Ms. Sharon thirty minutes to find him. When she found him she had a talk with him.

"I know it's been hard for you to get use to the orphanage and everything has changed for you in the past few months. What you did can never happen again", said

Sharon.

"Ok", replied James as he walked away.

"Come back here, I'm serious. We do not allow that kind of language here", Sharon added, "but I think I know something that may help. I don't know why I didn't think of this sooner".

Sharon left out the room and returned a few minutes later with a notebook.

"You have a lot of anger inside you which is understandable. For now on instead of yelling you can write your feelings down in here", said Sharon as she handed him the book. "This is your first and only warning. If this ever happens again your visits with

Sally will be taken away".

"Ok thanks", James said sarcastically as he walked out the room.

The next time Sally came to visit she was shocked to hear what happened. She knew he was upset but she didn't think he would use that kind of language. She thanked Sharon for allowing her to still see James after the incident.

"I think the book just might be working", said Sharon, "we haven't had any trouble out of him since I gave it to him".

"I'm pretty sure he was just having a bad day", Sally commented, "cause that doesn't sound like James at all, but thank for giving him the book".

"Oh you're more than welcome. Using the book to write feelings down has worked wonders in the past. James is really smart, one of the top students in all of his classes", said Sharon to Sally. "I just wish I'd thought of it sooner".

Later that day Sally didn't ask James about his out burst but she did ask him if the book helped. He told her it was but he still wanted to be left alone.

"I understand, but I can't be with you all the time. You need somebody your age to talk to, to do normal kid things with", said Sally.

Chapter 3
Danny

About a month later Danny came up to James and asked him what he thought about the orphanage.

"I'm still getting use to it", replied James.

"I've been here three years, I'm still not use to it", said Danny, "but I don't think I want to be".

"Three years, how have you done it all that time?" asked James.

"Come with me, I'll show you my

secret", answered Danny.

Danny took James to an area of the orphanage that James didn't know was there.

"This is where I come when I want to get away from everything", Danny added, "nobody knows about it so they can't find me until I want them to".

"I wish I had a place like this, I would never leave it", said James.

"I don't know about never coming out but you can share it with me if you want", said Danny.

"Are you sure. Why would you share this with me?" asked James.

"I don't know, there's just

something about you that tells me we can be good friends", answered Danny.

"Ok thanks. Can I come here anytime or just with you?" asked James.

"Whenever you want", replied Danny, "just keep it clean".

James and Danny were friends from that moment on. They spent almost all summer in their secret hideout. When they wasn't there, they were making fun of the other kids or getting into trouble some other way. Danny told James how he never knew his birth parents and how this was his second orphanage.

"I don't remember anything about the first one cause I was just a baby", explained Danny.

"So why did you come here?" asked James.

"Well I heard the other kids talking about how the first orphanage was old and falling apart", answered Danny, "so I think they moved some of us here and others somewhere else".

James told Danny stories of when his parents were still alive.
"My favorite parts of growing up was when my mom use to tell me stories every night", James said, "my dad tried after she died but it was never the same".
Even though Danny couldn't relate, it was one way he got to know James a little better. Danny didn't know how it felt to miss parents but

he did know what it felt like to be alone. Danny was younger than James so they had different classes. After class Danny and James did everything together.

The holidays were always the hardest for James, but Danny tried to do whatever he could to make James smile. When Christmas and birthdays came around James and Danny would always make special gifts for each other with whatever they could find at the orphanage. Danny even got to meet Sally on one of her visits. Sally was so happy that James found a friend.

"I'm glad you have someone to talk to and hang out with now, cause I have to go out of town for a little while to take care of my son", said Sally.

"Well I'm not glad that you have to go but I guess it's good I have Danny to keep me company while you're gone", replied James.

While Sally was away James and Danny became closer. James was even started calling Danny his best friend. James and Danny was always together until one day Danny was gone. Danny and James had talked about Danny getting adopted but they didn't know when he was leaving. Then one day Danny didn't show up to the secret hideout. When James talked to Ms. Sharon, she told him that Danny said it would've been too painful to say goodbye but he said he would call you later.

The next time Sally came to visit James was in a mood and didn't want to see anybody.

"I just came from seeing James. He looked sad, what happened?" Sally asked Sharon.

"His friend Danny got adopted a week ago and James went back into his shell", replied Sharon.

"He must be taking it really bad because he didn't even want to talk ", said Sally.

The next time Sally came to visit, James told her he felt alone since Danny left and nothing would ever be the same. Sally tried to console him by telling him that he'll make new friends but she knew he had lost too much. The next couple of weeks James thought about what Sally said about making new friends. James started talking to the other children, doing activities and he even talked to the staff a little more too. But he told Sharon he didn't want to get too close to anyone yet because he feared losing another friend. She understood where he was coming from and appreciated him trying.

One day Mr. & Mrs. Harrison came to McMichaelson Orphanage and Learning Center looking to adopt. As they looked around at all the children, talked to the staff and some of the children, they notice James all by himself. They looked at each other and then at Sharon,

"We would like to know more about that little fella over there in the corner", Mrs. Harrison said pointing at James.

"Well let go into my office and I'll tell you about him," Sharon replied. "I dont have much information on his parents. Just that both of them are deceased, James is his name. He's allergic to peanuts, otherwise very healthy. He's a little shy, a bit of a loner but very smart and wise for a 10 year old", Sharon told the Harrisons.

A little while later Sharon called James into her office,
 "James, I would like for you to meet Mr. & Mrs. Harrison. They're thinking about adopting and wanted to get to know some of the children", said Sharon as James entered the room.
Sharon stepped aside so James and the Harrisons could talk. The Harrisons asked James a couple of questions about himself and James

asked them some as well. Sharon was supprised that James somewhat opened up to the Harrisons but she didn't want to tell him they were interested in him just yet. After about twenty or thirty minutes Sharon asked James to step out of the room so she could talk to the Harrisons alone.

"If you're serious about adopting James, it will take us some time to get everything together, talk to James and his social worker", said Sharon.

"Take all the time you need, go through all the formality necessarily. We're sure we would like to adopt James", replied Mrs. Harrison.

About six months later, after doing a background check on the Harrison's, the Harrisons meeting with Mary's replacement Lisa, who told them that Mary didn't leave any information on James's parents. Sharon had a little talk with James.

"Do you remember a couple months ago when you met the Harrisons?" asked Sharon.

"Yes", answered James.

"What did you think of them?" asked Sharon".

"They were ok. They seemed nice. They made me feel almost as comfortable as when I first meet Sally. Why?" said James.

"Well that's good to hear because they're interested in adopting you," replied Sharon.

"Me, are you sure? They look like the type who would adopt someone younger," said James.

"Yes you, we still have a few more steps to take but they want to adopt you James," replied Sharon. "Never sell yourself short, you are a great young man with a lot of class and talent. Anyone would be lucky to have you as a son and if you decide to leave us you will be very much missed".

"I would have to get to know them a little more and Sally would have to be able to come see me there", replied James.

"Of course we can arrange that", said Sharon.

"Do you know if they have any other children?" asked James.

"I don't think so. They didn't say anything in our interview", said Sharon, "but you can ask them next time you see them".

And so he did along with a few others, like what did they do for a living and why did they decide to adopt an older child, just to name few.

"No other children, we're both retired and we are too old to be running around with a smaller child", answered Mr. Harrison.

"So what about you, do you have a favorite color, food, or things you like to do?" asked Mr. Harrison.

"Red, pizza, stories and board games," answered James, "the stories started when I was little. My mom use to tell me them every night. I guess it kind of stuck with me and the games came from my friend Sally. Well she's more like family. I would like y'all to meet her one day".

"We would love to", said Mrs. Harrison.

"So how's everything going?" asked Sally.

"Everything's fine, I think I want to go live with the Harrisons", James said.

"Is that so?" asked Sharon. "Are you sure?"

"Yes, I think so, why", said James.

"Its just you've been through a lot in your 11 years of life. This is a big decision and nobody want you to rush into anything", replied Ms. Sharon. "But if you're sure, we can go through with the rest of the steps and have the papers ready for them to sign in about four months. Do you think you can handle us for another couple months James?"

"I guess I will have to make do for that time period", James said.

For the next couple of months James seem very excited about leaving the orphanage. Sharon had to reminded him that even though he was happy to be leaving them, it might not be easy to started all over. She told him to just take it one day at a time and not to try and rush anything.

When the Harrison's came back to the orphanage to sign the papers they had a chance to meet Sally. Sally and the Harrisons talk for a while. The Harrisons learned a little about Sally, a little more about James. Sally learned about the Harrisons and where James would be living. They told Sally she was more than welcome to visit James once he got settled. After the Harrisons left Sally saw how happy James was to have new family. She just hope there was still room in his life for her.

Charter 4
Starting Over

July 1 1995, the Harrisons had come to pick James up. Sharon, Sally, Lisa and the rest of the orphanage were all there to say their goodbyes.

"I'll be checking in on you, so you be a good boy", said Sharon.

The whole way from the orphanage James thought about how he felt more comfortable with the Harrisons than he did in the three years at the orphange. He also thought about what Sharon said about starting over, which made him a little scared. So James just sat quiet for the rest of the ride. Once they got to the house James got the grand tour. Four bed rooms, two baths, living room, dining room, an attic, basement and the biggest kitchen James had ever seen. The last thing James saw was his room. It was painted white with red trim, with a bed and a big red chair. The Harrisons apologized that there wasn't anything else in his room but they wanted James to pick everything else he wanted out for himself. James felt a little nervous. He had never picked out furniture before. They went to three different stores to find everything James wanted for his room. The TV and the entertainment center was delivered the same day. The next day the dresser and side table was coming. James spent all day in his room with Mr. Harrison putting stuff together and fixing it up just the way he wanted. The only time they came down was when Mrs. Harrison called them to eat.

"Did you men have fun using your muscles up there?" asked Mrs. Harrison.

"Yes ma'am, we worked up a big appetite", replied James. "What's for dinner?"

"Pizza", said Mrs. Harrison, "you said that was your favorite right".

"Yes. But I was just wondering what do I call you now?" asked James.

"You can call us anything you feel comfortable with", answered Mrs. Harrison.

After they ate James and Mr. Harrison went back upstairs to put the finishing touches on the room. While they were working James told Mr. Harrison how his dad and him use to watch sports and movies together when he was home, but they never put anything together.

"You know we're not here to take the place or out do your parents right", said Mr. Harrison, "we just saw an unhappy child and thought we could bring happiness in his life".

"I'm sorry it came out like that", replied James, "I'm just trying to help you learn more about my past with my parents".

"Just don't rush it. We have the rest of the summer to get to know each other better", said Mr. Harrison.

He was almost right. This summer Mr. & Mrs. Harrison tryed to get James to talk and get to know them but it took a little more time than they thought. Then one day James asked Mrs. Harrison what did her and Mr. Harrison do before they retired.

"Well I use to be a school teacher, yep worked at the high school for 32 years", said Mrs. Harrison. "My husband worked at the bank for a little over 35 years, since before he graduated college. But he still tries to keep busy doing odd jobs here and there. I think he's just use to working. What did your parents do?"

"My dad worked at the steel plant

and my mom was a waitress", answered James.

That summer James got to see his new school, meet some of the teacher and got to know the neighborhood a little better. By the time school started James had even became friends with two of the nieghborhood kids.

The week before school started Mrs. Harrison and James reviewed some of his school work. He didn't like it but he wanted to be prepared for the 8 grade. James made sure he had everything ready for his first day at the new school. He even went to bed early the day before. When the alarm went off the next morning, James was already half dressed. A little later Mr. Harrison came to see if he was awake and to his surprise

James was on his way downstairs.

"Looks like we have ourself an early bird", said Mr. Harrison to James as they met in the hall.

"I didn't use to be. I guess that's just part of me growing up", James replied as he went down the stairs into the kitchen.

"Good morning sweety, are you ready for school?" asked Mrs. Harrison.

"As ready as I'm gonna be", replied James, "I think I'd like to walk to school today".

"If that's what you want", said Mrs. Harrison, "just make sure you don't forget anything".

So James ate his breakfast, gathered his things, told the Harrisons to have a good day and was off to school. James met up with his new friends at the corner and they decide to walk to school together. When James got to school he found out that his new friend, John was in his homeroom class. This made James feel a little better, at least he knew one person. The first day was a half day so James came home at one. Which was just in time for Sally's visit.

"Sorry I'm late, the boys and I were hanging around outside", said James as he walked in the door.

"That's ok", said Mrs. Harrison, "look who came for a visit".

James looked up, saw Sally, ran and gave her a big hug.

"How have you been? I thought you had forgotten about me", said James.

"I could never forget about you", replied Sally, "I told you I would let you settle in before I came to visit".

James showed Sally around the house and his room. He was so proud to say he picked everything out himself. James told her how big his school was, his friend John was in his class and all about the Harrisons.

"Good thing you're so good at school because after talking with Mrs. Harrison, I see she don't play", said Sally.

"Yea, I'm still trying to figure out if

it's a good thing or not to have an ex teacher as a mom", James said.

They talked so long Sally almost forgot that she had to pick up her medicine.

"Tell everyone I said goodbye", said Sally as she rushed out the door.

"Where was she off to in such a hurry?" asked Mr. Harrison.

"She had to get something from the store before it closed", answered James.

"So did you meet the any of your teacher yet?" asked Mr. Harrison.

"No we don't get our schedules until tomorrow", replied James. "Can I go outside?"

"Sure but change out of those school clothes first and be back for dinner", said Mr. Harrison.

The first couple of weeks of school James thought were easy because they were just reviewing what he already knew. As it got deeper into the school year James spent less time outside and more time studying and talking to Sally. By Thanksgiving break, James only went outside on the weekend.

One day while James was doing his homework the Harrison's asked him what he wanted to do for his birthday. He told them he would have to get back to them but he just didn't want to sound so eager. Later that week James went to Mrs. Harrison and said

"Ma, I've never had a real birthday party before, so do you think I could have one this year".

As she sat in awe because he had never called her ma before. James explained how when he was little his mother made him cakes and at the orphanage they had one party for everyone's birthday in that month.

"That was kind of fun but I've never had a birthday party for just me with my friends", said James.

"Well it looks like we're gonna have to give you your first birthday party", said Mrs. Harrison.

"My birthday is next month so I was wondering if y'all celebrated Christmas?" asked James.

"We use to before our son moved

out but now we just celebrate birthdays", replied Mrs. Harrison, "but we can start again if you want".

"No, that's ok I think Christmas is over rated, I'd rather feel special on my birthday", said James. "Wait did you say you had a son, where is he, how old is he?"

"We haven't talked to him in about, let's see, my memory is bad, it was a long time ago, at least fifteen years maybe more. He was one of the reasons I enjoyed being a teacher. He wasn't as good as you in school, but I enjoyed teaching him. It was a lot easier than the high schoolers. He should be around 40 now. I think you would've like him", answered Mrs. Harrison

"Do you have any pictures of

him?" asked James.

"There should be some around here somewhere. When I find them you'll be the first to know", said Mrs. Harrison, "come on now we have a party to plan".

Within the next few weeks they wrote out invitations, made arrangements for the cake, and James called Sally to invite her personally. The day of James's first birthday party he wanted everything to be perfect. He made sure the house was clean, there was room for everyone's coats. He even called everyone to make sure they would be there on time. As the guest arrived Mr. Harrison took everyone's coats and of course James took the presents. Everyone was having fun, Sally got to meet his friends, there was enough food and snacks for everyone. James was happy about the party. But he wished Danny could have been there. The time came to open gifts and James took time to thank everyone for every gift. When the party was over James had some new books, money, clothes, games and a new computer. Sally and a couple of the kids stayed behind to help clean up and play with James's new games. James had so much fun at the party he wanted to do the same next year.

With James's new computer and his mother being an ex teacher, James's 8 grade school year seemed to go by really quick. And easy once he learned how to put his work on a disk.

"Time went so fast, I can't believe

I've been living here for almost a years. In a few months I will be having my first graduation", said James.

"Well in honor of another of your first, what would you like to do for your graduation?" asked Mr. Harrison.

"We, meaning the boys and I thought if we got a few of the parents to help out, we could put our money together and go to a theme park for maybe three days", answered James.

"Well it's ok with me if it's ok with the other parents. I'll look online to start checking the prices later", said Mr. Harrison.

"Thanks dad", James said as he ran

out the door.

By the time graduation came the boys had done work around the nieghborhood and saved their money. Mike's parents had made hotel arrangements for themselves, James, his parents and John for three days, two nights at the theme park. John's parents were unable to go because they had younger children at home. While on their trip the boys had the time of their lives, especially since this was James's first time at a theme park. They went on almost all the rides, saw all the sights, and ate as much as they could. After their wonderful time was over the boys didn't want to go back home. Then they remembered they had the rest of the summer to hang out for free. As soon as they got back home James called Sally to tell her how much fun he had. They talked for a little while then Sally gave James a new mailing address and told him she was moving away to be closer to her children.

"We can write each other for a while until I get settled in", said Sally, "I want to hear all about your summer".

James had a busy summer from hanging out with Mike and John at the mall, going to movies, spending time with his parents and writing Sally. As Mike, John and James got ready for high school they made a pact, that they would still be friends. They would create a study group and always help each other out.

It was the first day of high school, at least for the 9th graders, but it was just orientation. They got a tour of the school, received their schedules and took their school ID photo. The boys had English, math and lunch together which was funny because James was good at English, John was good at math and Mike loved to eat.

Chapter 5
Hidden Treasure

High school was different and harder than what they were use to. John, Mike and James knew they had to work hard after getting homework their first week. Mike and John made James the leader of the study group, because he was the better student. James made sure they did all their school work before they went anywhere or had any fun. As much as Mike and John hated it they knew it was what they needed. Mike, John and James didn't do any school activities or spend any time outside, except for on breaks or when James's parents told them they were studying to hard. During their first two years of high school, Mike and John spent so much time at the Harrison's, their parents thought they had moved in. By the end of their sophomore year the boys added three new members to the study group. They only studied with them on the weekend. Everyone said James had a crush on the new girl Tonya but he always denied it. All the hard work paid off. Well at least for James, who got an early acceptance to college at the age of 15. But he needed more credits, plus he didn't wanna leave home or his friends and felt he would be better prepared for college in a couple more years.

One night when all the studying was over Mr. Harrison came to talk to James.

"You know I was shy when I met your mother", said Mr. Harrison, "maybe if you try to get to know each other, you two might have a lot in common".

"Who Tonya, she's just my friend, like one of the guys", replied James, "but Tonya does like games and movies".

"Just think on it, you got a lot of time, no rush", said Mr. Harrison.

"Ok, good night dad, give mom a kiss for me and tell her I said good night", said James.

James thought long and hard about what his father said, but he was a little scared. He had never been this close with a girl before. He didn't wanna mess up whatever friendship he could have with Tonya. James didn't know how to be a boyfriend. He barely knew how to be a regular friend.

The next day Mr. Harrison asked James had he given any thoughts to what he wanted to do after graduation.

"I'm not sure what I want to be when I grow up yet", replied James. "But I don't think I want to go straight to college either. I thought I might find a job and try to save up some money for college first".

"I'm glad you have a plan, most people don't", said Mr. Harrison. "You know anything you need your mother and I will help right".

"Yes, but you've already given me so much and y'all have this big house to take care of", said James.

"Well actually the house is paid in full. It was your mother's parents", said Mr. Harrison. "All we pay is utilities and food. The taxes is paid up for the next four years. Plus Nancy's mother left her a nice chunk of change when she died five years ago, so you don't have to work so hard".

"That's good to know but I still don't think I'll be going to college right out of high school", said

James.

The summer had came and went. It was almost time for school to start, but Mike and John were mad at James.

"We barely saw you or got to do anything together this summer", said John with an angry tone, "everytime we called your mother said you were with Tonya".

"What is she your girlfriend now?" added Mike.

"Yes", replied James, "do y'all have a problem with that?"

"No, we just missed hanging out with you", said John.

"Yea, but we don't want no funny

business in our study group", said Mike.

"Well you know nothing's messing with my school work", said James.

This school year was different for the boys and not just because James had a girlfriend. Mike played football, John played basketball and James volunteered at the Big Brother after school program. The only person James saw everyday was Tonya. When they wasn't together they were on the phone.

"So Big Brother, what made you decide to volunteer there?" asked Mrs. Harrison.

"Well I heard they helped young boys stay out of trouble, with school work and stuff", replied James. "I thought why not give back, after all I've been given. I start Monday after school, plus I can use this for the credits I need to graduate".

"Just make sure you keep up your grades and be home everyday for dinner", said Mrs. Harrison as James walked up the stairs.

Later that day around dinner time the phone rang, "its Tonya", said Mrs. Harrison as she held the phone for James, "don't be too long, your food will get cold".

Two minutes later James came back in the kitchen,

"She just wanted to know if I could to go to the movies tomorrow", James mumbled as he ate his food, "I can go right".

"Yes, you two have been spending a lot of time together", said Mr. Harrison, "what it been now six months?"

"No, its only been two but it does feel like longer", James said, "I really like her, we have a lot in common and we have fun together".

The next day James went to the movies with Tonya and when he returned he was extra excited.

"What you so happy for?" asked Mr. Harrison.

"My relationship with Tonya has gone to a new level", said James.

"I won't tell your mother about this but I was around your age the first time I had sex", said Mr. Harrison nudging James with his elbow.

"What no! Remember when I told you Tonya and I had a lot in common", said James. "Tonya told me she was adopted too but when she was a baby and she wants me to meet her parents tomorrow".

"Oh well that's great too", said Mr. Harrison. "I didn't meet your mother parents until after our first year together. That's a big step. Are you sure your ready for this".

"Is he ready for what? Y'all better not be talking about sex", said Mrs. Harrison as she entered the room.

"No, what's wrong with you two", replied James, "I'm going to meet Tonya's adopted parents tomorrow".

"Adopted, ain't she a little too old for that?" asked Mrs. Harrison.

"See Nancy, that's what you get for coming in at the end of a conversation", said Mr. Harrison. "James just found out that Tonya was adopted as a baby".

"Oh, that is a big step, but I'm sure they're going to love you. Unlike when my parents met Mike, they didn't like him at first", said Mrs Harrison, "it might've had something to do with me being pregnant but that's a story for another time".

"I think I've learned enough about you two for one day", said James, "I'm going to my room".

The next day at noon James was just

waking up.

"What time do you meet the parents? "Are you ready?" asked Nancy.

"I'm going over there at 4 and I'm a little nervous. But Tonya and I agreed that we wouldn't let their feelings for me mess up our relationship", replied James.

Nancy and James talked a little longer then James went upstairs to get ready. An hour later James was off to meet Tonya's parents. While James was away Nancy and Mike did some fall cleaning. In doing so they found some old photos and some of their son's things. When James came home he told his parents all about Tonya's house and parents. How their house reminded him of his old neighborhood, her parents were nice, they asked him a lot of questions and wanted to met them one day. He learned a little more about Tonya, like she loves stuffed animals, allergic to raw tomatoes and she has never had a pet. Which was another thing they had in common.

"I'm going to sleep now, I have big day tomorrow", said James.

The next day James went to school and then to the Big Brothers program. When he came home his parents wanted to know all about his day.

"Well school was school", James said, "the Big Brother program was fun, I meet some of the kids. We played games and did school work. I spent time with some of the other volunteers. Some of them had been with the program for ten years".

"We're glad you enjoyed yourself, maybe you can rub some of your intelligence off on the young ones", said Mr. Harrison.

The next few months were very busy for James with school, Big Brothers, family, Tonya and planning this years birthday party. Tonya and James spent most of their free time together, getting to know each other and just hanging out. Tonya and James was each other first boyfriend\girlfriend, so everything relationship wise was new to them. They spent a lot of time at each others house, playing games, having dinner and watching movies. Comedies and action were their favorite. But everything went from good to bad over a homework assignment. James came home from school early and when his mother asked why, he went straight upstairs and slammed the door. Later he came down, he was still upset but explained what was wrong.

"I'm just upset because we have to make a family tree for class and my teacher didn't want to hear how my parents were dead, I was adopted and never knew any of my relatives", James explained.

"I'll go up to the school tomorrow to see if I can help", said Mrs. Harrison. "I have something I hope will make your day a little better. Mike and I was cleaning and we found some of our son's things".

When she came back in the room she had a box. In the box was a baseball trophy, some report cards, a birth certificate, pictures and other little things.

"Wow that's a big trophy", said James, "what was that for?"

"I think it was the championship, I don't remember what year, the gold plate must've fell off", replied Nancy.

"He wasn't that bad in school, he had a C average on most of these", James commented as he looked at the report cards.

James went on looking through the box, then all of a sudden stopped and said he had to go upstairs. After about thirty minutes Nancy called him to see if he was ok, there was no answer. When she went upstairs to his room, he was on his bed full of paper.

"You ok?" she asked.

He lifted his head up with a confused look on his face.

"Just so I'm clear, is this your son?" James asked handing her a picture.

"Yes, but where did you find it", she replied.

"Are you sure the man in that picture is your son?" James asked once again.

"Yes, I don't know the lady but that is definitely my son Tom", Nancy replied.

"Well I didn't find the picture, it's

the only photo I have of my mom and dad", said James.

"Are you telling me what I think you're telling me?" Nancy asked after a long silence.

"Yes, I think you're my grandma", James said in a calm voice.

"Oh my goodness, I didn't know Tom had a kid", Nancy shouted.

"When I heard your last name at the orphanage I didn't think anything of it because Harrison is a common name. Then when you said you had a son I never put two and two together", said James.

Some time went past before Nancy spoke again. But before she did tears dropped from her eyes.

"What wrong mom?" asked James.

"As excited as I am that you're blood, I'm also sad because if you're my grandson that means my Tom is dead", answered Nancy.

"Oh I'm sorry I never thought about it that way", James said while giving his mother a hug. "Is there anything I can do to make you feel better".

"Not right now, I just need sometime to myself", Nancy said. "Just out of curiosity, how did he die?"

"He had stage four lung cancer. It spreaded to both lunges and he died about a two weeks after he learned the news. If it helps the hospital made him very comfortable", James replied.

Later that day when Mike returned home James told him what happened and that his mother had been in her room ever since. Mike sat there for a while with a strange look, then said he would go check on her and gave James some money to order pizza. Nancy felt little better over time as James told them stories about how his father was when he was alive.

Chapter 6
Transition

On Monday when James went to school he told Mike, Tonya and John that his adoptive parents turned out to be his grandparents. Then when the people at the Big Brother program asked what happened to him, he just had to tell the whole story all over again. But James wasn't the only person talking, so was Nancy.

"Well I was telling Maggie, you know John's mother, about our grandson", Nancy said, "and she said we should get a blood test done, so we could have paperwork. Do you think you can miss another day at the Big Brother program tomorrow, seeing that you have a half day at school?"

"I guess, I just have to call Keith(the guy in charge at the center)", replied James.

"Now about this blood test. Do they need both of our blood or does you being his grandma make me his grandpa by default?" asked Mike.

"Yes they need your blood because last time I checked you were still Tom's father. It will just be a prick, stop being a baby", replied Nancy.

"That's ok dad I don't like needles either", James added as he patted him on the shoulder.

"You know I couldn't love you any more than I already do, cause you're already family", said Mike.

"I know I feel the same way dad", said James.

Everyone went to bed that night with plans of getting a blood test the next day. The first thing Mike said when he woke up was can they just use the blood sample they have at the doctor office.

"Its too early for this", Nancy mumbled, "but no they can't because they use that blood to do their own tests. Besides you can't walk up in there with a val of blood looking like a crazy person".

Everyone went their separate ways, all agreeing to meet back at the house by two. Later they went to take the test and Mike didn't say a word all the way there. But to his surprise they didn't need his blood. They just took a swab from his cheek for the DNA test. The doctor said it would take two to three weeks for the test to come back. So everyone went on with their daily duty which included planning James's seventeenth birthday party.

At the party Mike, John and James spent time catching up and making plans to try to hang out more that summer. James's parents got a chance to finally meet Tonya's parents. They hit it off well. For James's birthday this year he received money, a cell phone, a new wallet, cards and more money. His grandparents also told him about the trust fund they made for him, that he couldn't get until he was eighteen.

"We started it about a month after you came to live with us", explained

Mike, "it's yours to do whatever you wanted to do with it later".

Days after the party James learned more about his father. Mike told him that Tom got suspended from school at least fifteen times of his thirteen years.

"Mostly for fighting, some for skipping classes and others just because he didn't do what he was told", Mike explained.

"While on the subject of my dad, did he have a trust fund too?" asked James.

"Yes", replied Mike, "but he wasn't smart with it. See Tom had no plans of going to college. He spent his money on partying with friends. Yea your dad loves to hang out and drink with his friends even before he was legally able to".

"Y'all let him!" said James.

"Well the first time I caught him he was eighteen. We had a long talk about the dangers of drinking and how people make bad decisions when they're drunk", said Mike. "He said he was smarter than that and he didn't drink often or that much".

"You didn't do anything to make him stop?" asked James.

"I actually learned early in his life that the more I didn't want him to do something the more he was going to do it", answered Mike. "But everything changed the day after his twenty first birthday".

"Why?" asked James.

"He got so drunk that he was either in the bed or the bathroom for three days", said Mike. "He told us he would never drink again".

"Did he keep his word. When I was little my mom told me he got drunk in a bar, hurt someone and was in jail until I was four months old", James explained, "but I don't remember him drinking as I grew up".

"I don't know for sure we lost contact. But you know some people always have to learn the hard way", replied Mike. "I'm going to let you get some sleep now. I would love to hear more about your father one day".

"Ok, goodnight grandpa. I just wanted to see what it sound like", said James.

The next week James went to school and returned home about four.

"What are you doing home so early?" asked Nancy.

"The centers is being painted, so we don't have the program for the next couple of days", answered James.

"Well I'm glad you're home, our test came back today", said Nancy.

"What test?" inquired James.

"Our DNA test we took to prove that you're blood related", replied

Nancy.

"Ok, just for the fun of it, what does it say", said James.

"It says Mr. Smarty Pants, that I've been raising my grandson for the last four years", said Nancy.

James sat there with a strange look on his face. To him the piece of paper didn't matter, they were already family. But he knew it meant something to his mother.

As the summer came the boys spent a little more time together, while they filled out college applications, took the A.C.T. and prepared for their senior year in high school. James and Tonya also celebrated their one year anniversary. Nothing big just went to a movies and out to dinner. Everyone was so excited to be going to the twelth grade. They knew this year would be the best yet. James didn't wanna tell anyone just yet that he wasn't going to college like the rest of them. He didn't know how they would take it and he wasn't for sure if his grandmother knew or not yet.

The twelth grade was more like the ninth grade to James and the boys, hard. They really didn't have their study group last year but they tried to get back into it at the library. Even though James wasn't going to college, he still wanted to get his grades back up. Beside his mother wouldn't have it any other way. Seeing how James was studying so hard to keep his grades up he didn't volunteer at the Big Brother program this year.

One day as James returned from school his mother asked him what he wanted to do for his birthday.

"Well since I'll be 18, I thought I would just hang out with my friends", James said. "You and dad have done so much for me already. I think you two need a break. I'm getting too old for birthday parties, it's time for me to grow up".

"Look at my little man, too old for parties. Next thing I know you'll be off to college, living your own life, with a family of your own", replied Nancy.

James paused for a second before saying another word.

"Now don't get too carried away. All of that will happen in time. You're not getting rid of me that easy. I'm not going to college right after I graduate", said James.

"What was that now?" asked Nancy.

"I've been in school or taught all my life. I don't want to just go off to college just because that's what everyone else is doing", said James. "If I do go I at least want to have a goal and right now I don't know what I want to be".

"So what are you going to do after graduation?" asked Nancy.

"Hopefully, I'll be working next summer. I was thinking about somewhere in the mall", replied

James.

"You have grown into a very smart young man. Your parents would have been very proud of you", Nancy said as she walked away with tears in her eyes.

James sat there for a while before he got up and went after her.

"Since we're on the topic of things that's happening next year, maybe you can help me out with something", said James.

"Sure I can try, what's up", Nancy replied.

"Well you know how much I care for Tonya right? Well we'll be together for two years in August and I wanna start planning our anniversary now, but I don't know what to do", James explained.

"Well jewelry always works. Have you asked Tonya what she wanted to do?" asked Nancy.

"No, she's always been a "go with the flow" type of person. I didn't think about that, thanks", said James as he walked out the room.

Dinner time came and Nancy was still feeling some type of way about the conversation she had with James earlier.

"Mike, did you know that James was not going to college after he graduates?" asked Nancy.

"Yes, he wants to work and figure everything out first and I think its a great idea", answered Mike.

"Well did you know", Nancy started.

"Yes I also knew he didn't wanna have a birthday party this year", Mike interrupting, "would you let the boy grow up, he's a good kid. Just because he doesn't want a party doesn't mean he doesn't love you or you did anything wrong".

"Mom, you don't actually think that do you. I love you and I love everything you do for me. That's one of the reasons I decided to go off this year. I thought you should take some time to yourself", James stated. "If you want you can make me breakfast but your gift to me will be to treat yourself to a day at the spa".

The next couple of weeks James tried hard to make is mother feel special. He brought her flowers, helped around the house and tried to get her to relax as much as possible. Seeing how happy it made her, James started thinking about his anniversary again. He still planned to do whatever Tonya wanted to do but with a special surprise.

The week before James's birthday, Nancy asked James what he wanted for his birthday breakfast.

"Eggs, bacon, French toast, Oj and some strawberry jam if we have any", James answered.

"Ok then, I thought you wanted me to relax. If that's all you want, I guess that's what you'll have",

Nancy replied as she walked out of the room.

The morning of his birthday James woke up to the aroma of breakfast. He quickly washed up, got dressed and ran downstairs just as Nancy was putting his plate on the table.

"That smells so good I almost came downstairs in my pajamas", said James, "hope you made enough for everybody".

"None for me dear, I have some errands to run", said Mike as he walked around the house, "happy birthday James".

James ate his breakfast, then finished getting ready for school.

"Will you be home after school?"

asked Nancy.

"Yes, the guys and I aren't hanging out until about six", replied James as he walked out the door.

After James left Nancy sat at the table eating some French toast and bacon. Then she did the dishes, tided up a little and relaxed for the rest of the day. When Mike came home he was surprised to see Nancy was sitting down in the living room.

"So what did you do today?" he asked.

"I gave James his birthday wish. I didn't go to a spa but I relaxed and took the day off. I really enjoyed myself", she replied. "What about you, did you get all your errands ran?"

"Yes I did, but it was hard to find a birthday card that says exactly how I feel", said Mike. "I think I would've had better luck making an old school card by hand".

So for the rest of the day Nancy and Mike relaxed. This was different for Mike cause he was use to being busy. They were so relaxed that they fell asleep before James returned home from school. When James came home and saw they were asleep, he didn't wake them. Then he saw an envelope on the table with his name on it. He picked it up and opened it. It was a card that read "happy birthday grandson", inside it was $100 and some words that he didn't read. It was signed grandma and grandpa with love. James thought he would thank them later.

He went in the kitchen, got him something to eat and went upstairs to get ready to go out. By the time he came downstairs his girlfriend Tonya was there talking to his grandparents. He gave them both a hug and kiss and thanked them for the card before walking out the door. Tonya and James met the rest of their friends at the bowling alley. They bowled a few rounds before going to a movie and grabbing something to eat. James came home about eleven and told his grandparents all about his night. They were so happy he had a great time. Nancy didn't feel bad about him not having a big party anymore.

The next morning at the breakfast table Nancy asked James what did he spend his money on.

"Nothing, my friends paid for everything last night. I put my all birthday money in my bank", replied James.

"All your birthday money. How much did you get?" she asked.

"I'm not telling, next thing I know you'll be wanting to borrow some money", answered James in a joking tone, "and I got prom to prepare for".

"Very funny young man, have a nice day at school", she replied as James walked to the front door.

So his birthday was over but the next couple of month would be busy. Not only for James but the rest of his friends and classmates as well. For starters the school didn't have a senior trip this year. Instead they had a carnival/talent show to raise money for new uniforms for the basketball and football team. While most of the seniors were very upset, James and his friends were fine. They were saving their money for prom anyway. During the talant show Tonya sang a little while John and Mike did a dance routine. James didn't think he had any talent so he just sold his mother's cookies on the side. After some of the parents chipped in and the other students did their parts, the school had raised a little over what they needed for the uniforms. The rest they put up just in case the seniors needed extra money for prom.

A couple of weeks later, the school held their Mott election for the senior class. Somehow James and Tonya were tied for best couple with a couple that had been together for about four years. James, John and Mike won best crew, Tonya won best smile and James won most likely to sucessed. The gang had fun with everything. They walked around school like they all just won Grammy's. After taking their finals they all were looking forward to senior skip day. All the seniors met up at the park and had a big bar b que before everyone went their own ways. At the park everyone talked about prom, who they were taking and what they were wearing.

Between looking for a suit and Tonya finding the perfect dress, Tonya and James had little time to talk.

"I know we will be busy with

graduation and you have your college prep to do but I was wondering what you wanted to do for our two year anniversary?" asked James.

"I have to think on that for a while but wait you said I have college prep not we, you're not going to college", Tonya said with concern in her voice.

"No, not right away. So did you pick a college yet", James replied trying to change the subject.

"So why didn't you tell me this last summer, when we were all talking about colleges and our futures after high school?" she asked.

"I didn't know how y'all would take it. With me getting early acceptance two years ago, I thought y'all might think I was crazy and try to make me change my mind", answered James.

"I don't know about the guys, but I would never try to make you change how you feel as long as you're sure that's what you want to do", said Tonya. "So what are your plans after you graduate?"

"Well I'll be working this summer. Don't know where yet but I'm hoping somewhere in the mall. I think my interviews went good", replied James. "While working I'll think of the next steps in my life".

"When are you going to tell the guys. Do your parents, grandparents know?" asked Tonya.

"I'll tell the guys eventually and yes

my grandparents know", answered James. "They want to be known as my grandparents now. I think it's their way of staying connected to my father".

"On another note, what color is your suit for prom?" asked Tonya, "I'm not try to match you cause I think that's chessey but I do want our colors to look nice together".

"I think it's going to be blue. I have a choice between two suits I like. One is blue and the other is like a redish color", replied James.

"Yea, you should get the blue one cause I really like this red dress I saw the other day. Red and blue looks good together right" said Tonya.

"Yes" replied James. "Would you look at the time, my grandparents will be calling me soon if I'm not home for dinner. I'll talk to you later and don't forget to let me know what you want to do for our anniversary".

"Ok I will, as soon as I know you'll know. See you later", Tonya said before giving James a kiss on the lips.

After dinner James went to his grandfather to ask some advice.

"How did you know when the right time was to tell grandma you loved her?" asked James.

"Well first you have know if you really feel that way", Mike started.

"I really think I do. She's the first

thing I think of when I wake up, the last thing I think of on my way to sleep", James interrupted, "when I'm with her I never want to leave. I don't think I can ever get tired of seeing her face or being around her".

"So if you do love her what's holding you up from telling her. Do you think she feels the same?" asked Mike.

"I think she do, but I think we're both scared to say it first for fear of rejection", answered James.

"Well you two have been together for a while now and I've seen how y'all are together. I can only tell you to take the chance and tell her how you feel", said Mike. "If you really think she feels the same, go for it. I think your relationship will last even if she don't feel the same yet".

"Your right, I'm will probably think on it little more but I will tell her how I feel and give her as much time as she needs to say it back. I love Tonya and I'm not going anywhere", James shouted.

"Ok then, good talk, I'm going to bed now", Mike said.

Time had passed and the night before prom had arrived. James sat in his room by himself thinking of all the talks with his grandparents, his future and how everything is right around the corner. Mike walked in and asked why he looked so sad.

"Well I was thinking about the next couple of weeks", replied James, "after prom comes graduation then I will actually be out in the real world. Even though I've made plans and I am mostly prepared, it still will be different with my friends going their separate ways".

"Well that's all part of growing up but if you're really as close of friend as I think y'all are, you will find time to keep in touch with each other", explained Mike. "Most teens either go to college or get a job after graduation, you will be just fine".

"You're right I guess I'll see my friends every so often. I'll still be here on their breaks", said James. "Tomorrow is a big day so I'm going to sleep now, good night".

"Ok, good night", said Mike.

The next day James slept until noon, got a hair cut and started getting ready for prom about 6pm. Since they were all going together John, Mike, his date and Tonya met at the Harrison's house to take pictures before they left in the limo that Mike's parents rented. Everyone looked so nice especially Tonya with her nice fitted red dress with her hair put back. Mike and John looked like pengins in their rented tuxedos. They had to pick up John's date then it was off to prom. At the prom they had a great time, they laughed, ate, danced, took more pictures and reminisced. John and Mike were surprised that James wasn't going to college after graduation. They were sure he was going to college with Tonya. James returned home around three the next morning after dropping Tonya off.

Once again his grandparents went to sleep while waiting up for him.

The next morning James woke up feeling sick, he thought it was something he ate at the prom. That was until his friends called and told him someone spiked the punch with alcohol last night. They all promised not to tell their parents about it, as far they knew it was food poisoning. Since they had no classes after finals James, Tonya, John and Mike hung out as much as they could. Tonya told the guys she was going to school to become a registered nurse. Mike planned to go to community college, unsure what he was going to major in and John also decided he was going to work for a couple of years to help out his family.

Chapter 7
The Real World

June 12, 2001, graduation day had came,

"Are you ready for the real world?" Mr. Harrison asked James.

"I'm ready to start my job and start thinking about my future, but I don't think I'm ready to stop hanging out with my friends", replied James.

"Well you still have two weeks until you start your job don't you?" asked Mr. Harrison.

"Yea, but Mike's going to pick his dorm room in a week and I'm not sure when Tonya's leaving", said James.

"Why is Mike leaving so early, he's going to a commuity college right?" asked Mr. Harrison.

"Yes, but he wants to stay on campus. He wanted to make sure he had a good dorm room and job before everyone arrives in the fall", replied James.

"I'm so proud of you", Mrs. Harrison said as she walked into the room, "I always knew this day would come. It just came so quick, I should've been more prepared".

"Grandma I'm just graduating, I'm still going to be here for a couple more years", James said.

"I know but you've just grown up so fast, right before our eyes. I know its only been five years but I feel like I've raised you since birth", Mrs. Harrison started. "I'm just happy that I get to share this moment with you, I know your parents would be proud".

"We won't get to share anything with him if we just keep talking about it. We all need to get up and get ready, James you more than anyone. You have to be at the auditorium in less than an hour", Mr. Harrison said in a serious tone.

"Ok grandpa, my clothes are already set out, I just have to jump in the shower and I'll be ready to go", said James.

They all went in separate directions

and prepared for graduation. James got ready and left out twenty minutes later, telling his grandparents that he would see them later.

As all the parents gathered into the building Mike's mom Janet pull Nancy to the side.

"I was looking at the program and I didn't see James's name with the H's. Is that right?" Janet asked.

"Oh yes, James decided to keep Peterson, his mother's last name", Nancy replied.

"That was nice and sweet of him, come on Tonya's parents saved all of us seats", said Janet.

As the parents, guardians, family

and friends took their seats, the graduating class lined up to take theirs. After all the hooping, cheering and screaming subsided the principal began speaking. Later she introduce the guest speaker, then the valedictorian spoke. Awards, scholarships and plaques were given out. About two hours later the students crossed the stage, which came with a lot of tears from family and friends as well as the graduates. After it was all said and done, James had 4 plaques and 3 awards; Tonya had 2 awards and 2 plaques; Mike and John also had 2 awards each. But the best was yet to come for James. As everyone went home planning to meet up later for dinner, James returned home to find his graduation gift, a red 1998 Thunderbird.

"Wow thanks! I love it but you know I don't have a drivers license right", said James.

"Yes dear, but as busy as you've been these days you would've never gotten around to it. So we thought we'd give you a reason to get one", replied Nancy.

"If you want I can teach you to drive before you take your tests, no rush just whenever you're ready", added Mike.

"Ok that would be great. I'll let you know once I get my work schedule together. Thanks again, I love you! Wait until I tell the guys", shouts James in excitement as he went in the house to change.

First person he called was Tonya, to

tell her that he had a car.

"But you don't have a drivers license", she said.

"My first words exactly. My grandfather said he would teach me and when I get time I can take the written test", replied James.

"Now that I have you on the phone I know what I want to do for our anniversary", Tonya started.

"When do you leave for school?" James interrupted.

"I don't start school until September", said Tonya.

"This day just keeps getting better and better. Oh I'm sorry, I'm just so happy about everything, what were you saying", said James.

"Well I was saying, that for our two year anniversary I would like to have a nice dinner, just the two of us. Where we exchange gifts", Tonya continued, "nothing fancy, just something to show how we feel about each other".

"That will be great. I already have a couple of ideas in mind. I'm about to finish getting ready, I'll see you later", said James.

"Ok, can't wait for you to see the restaurant my parents picked out, you're gonna love it", Tonya said.

Before James could finish getting undressed he had a strange feeling that something was missing. He took a seat in his chair and thought about how he would have loved more than everything for his parents to be alive today. How they would have been proud of him and all his achievements. James started to feel real sad thinking about how he missed his parents and how he hope he made them proud. Then he thought that only in a perfect world could his parents still be alive and at the same time he was able to know his grandparents. James sat there for a while with tears running down is face until his grandmother called up to see if he was ready.

"Almost, I'll be down in a minute", James replied as he wiped his face.

A little while later James, Tonya, Mike, John, their parents, John little brother and sister all met at an all you can eat Italian buffet. While there James told the guys about his new car; how he was going to get his license this summer and how he wanted them to spend as much time together before everyone got too busy.

"We are still going to be in the states James. It's not like when we go to college we're gonna drop off the face of the planet. There's always weekends, holidays and telephone calls", said Mike.

"Yea James, I'll be still in the neighborhood and Tonya's not leaving for a whole three months. Stop being so sensitive, let eat", added John.

For the rest of the night the gang spent their time talking bout how they met each other. Mike was the first to meet James because he lived two doors down from the Harrisons.

His mother was noisy and had to see what was going on. John already knew James was coming because Nancy and John's mom had been friends for years. Tonya through it was funny that she had known Mike and John for years though school but never really talked to them until high school. James told them how he was scared to become friends with them at first because of his past with Danny, but was very glad he did.

"You've mentioned this Danny before, who is he?" asked John.

"Danny was my one and only friend at the orphanage. He was always there for me. Although he was younger, he helped me when I felt alone. He was a true friend. I haven't been that close to anyone else until I met you guys", James replied.

"So what happened to him?" asked Mike.

"He got adopted about a year before I did and we lost contact", answered James.

Mike and John tried to lighten the mood by talking about the time they went to the theme park and tried to pick up girls. But James got mad and took Tonya to another area. While away from the others, Tonya's father came over to talk to James and Tonya.

"Sorry to interrupt y'all dinner. I just wanted to tell y'all that Mrs. Powers and I are so proud of you two", said Mr. Powers. "When the guest speaker was talking about bright kids that will go far, I could only think of you two".

"I was raised right, learned life lessons from you and mom, I owe all my accomplishments to y'all, so thanks dad", said Tonya.

"My daughter's going out into the real world now, that means you have to look out for her now James", said Mr. Powers, "I'm putting my only child's life in your hands, don't let me down".

"I'll always look out for Tonya, always have and always will, you have nothing to worry about Mr. P", replied James.

"Ok, I'll be watching", said Mr. Powers as he walked away.

On their way back over to John and Mike, Tonya told James she was glad that her dad didn't say anything about college because she didn't tell them that he wasn't going. They got back to the table to find that Mike and John's parents had did the same as Tonya's dad.

"See that's why I talk to my grandparents all the time so they don't have to embarrass me in public", said James, "they did all that this morning before graduation". They spent a little more time talking. John told them he got the job at the shoe store. They were proud and glad for him. James told them that he start his job at the Chocolate Palace in two weeks. By the time the night was over they were all looking forward to not seeing each other for a couple of days, even though Mike was leaving for college next week.

The next month or so James spent all his time trying to make plans for Tonya and his anniversary. He kept everything a secret. Everytime his grandmother asked he would always say you'll know once Tonya knows. August 10, the two year anniverary of Tonya and James had finally came. Luckily James was able to get that day off work. Once again Nancy tried to get something out of James about what he had planned. Again he said nothing as he walked out of the door, to the car. Where his grandfather waited to take him to pick up Tonya. Once they picked her up, James gave Tonya flowers and gave his grandfather direction to where they were having dinner.

"I know you might've been thinking of dinner in a restaurant.

But this is the park my mom and I use to walk pass everyday. We thought it would be nice to have a picnic here, but we never did", explained James as they exited the car.

"Oh this is perfect, I had no where special I wanted to go, as long as I'm with you, I'm great", said Tonya.

"Thanks granddad, I'll call you to pick us up later and don't tell grandma. I want to tell her the whole story when I get home", James said.

"Don't worry I won't, I know how your grandmother likes your stories", replied Mike as he drove away.

Tonya and James found the perfect spot for their picnic, under a big tree, away from all the kids playing. James laid the blanket on the grass, then asked Tonya if she wanted to exchange gifts first.

"It depends on whether the food is hot or cold", answered Tonya.

"I thought you might say that and because I knew I wasn't going to be able to wait to give you your gift, we have sea food salad, sandwiches and your favorite juice from when we first started dating. For dessert chocolate cake", said James.

"All my favorites, you know me so well, that's why I love you", Tonya said before she realize what came out out her mouth.

"I love you too", James said without missing a beat.

They both sat there with smiles on their faces, thinking of how that was the first time they had said those word to each other or anyone other than their parents. Then James went into the basket and pulled out a necklace with a charm on it that said "I love you".

"This was the way I was planning on telling you how I felt. So if you didn't feel the same you could've just took the charm off until you did", James explained as he put the necklace on Tonya.

"Oh I love it! How could you ever think I didn't love you?" Tonya asked as she looked at the necklace.

"Don't know, I never had a girlfriend before, so I just didn't want to rush you into anything. I knew I would've still loved you and I would've waited until you felt the same about me", replied James.

They sat there, ate, kissed and talked for another hour or two before James called his grandfather to come pick them up. They really wasn't ready to leave. They had just watched a beautiful sun set, but they didn't want their parents to worry or get the wrong ideas. While waiting for his grandfather, Tonya told James that her parents wasn't too happy when she told them that he wasn't going to college.

"I know, they just want the best for you. But I don't think I would be the best for you or myself if I just went to college without having any plan of what I wanted to do", said James.

"That would be a waste of time and money".

"That's what I told them. Who cares what they think, not everyone's meant to go to college", Tonya replied.

After dropping Tonya off James went home and told his grandparents all about his lovely evening.

"See what did I tell you? There's no point in being scared to tell the ones you love how you feel", said Mike.

"I'm so happy for you two. You guy make the cutest couple", said Nancy, "what was your gift from Tonya?"

"She gave me a gold pocket watch with a picture of her on the inside and "with you always" engrave on the back", replied James.

"That's nice, well goodnight guys. I just stayed up to be noisy", said Nancy.

"Goodnight grandma, I'll be going to bed soon myself", said James, "after I call Tonya".

"That will be a couple of hours. I'll be up in a minute hun", said Mike.

For the next couple of months James seemed to always be on the phone. Either he was talking to Mike at school, John, or Tonya at school. Between him on the phone, at work or with Tonya, his grandparents only saw or talked to him when his grandfather was teaching him to drive. They didn't even know what he was planning to do for his ninteenth birthday, but neither did he. With everyone either in school or working James really didn't think of anything to do cause he didn't know who would be free. Little did he know he didn't have to cause his friends had already planned to surprise him. The weekend of January 6 had came around, Tonya, Mike and John had all cleared their schedules for the weekend, met up at James's house and waited for him to get off work. James returned home from work to tell his grandparents that his co-workers threw him a party.

"That was very nice of them, let's go in the kitchen so you can tell us all about it", said Mrs. Harrison.

Nancy, Mike and James walked into

the kitchen, as James turned the corner he saw Tonya, Mike and John.

"What are you guys doing here?" asked James.

"We came to spend the weekend with you for your birthday. Surprise!" replied Mike.

"Did y'all arrange this with my boss. This is only the third weekend I've had off since I've started working there?" asked James.

"Actually no, but we were hoping that you would have it off", said Tonya.

"So we're all together for the weekend. What are we going to do?" asked James.

"You're asking a lot of questions, just go with the flow. All you need to know is that we're all staying here for the weekend and we're going have a good time", said John.

That they did. The next three days was like a big sleep over. Tonya and James had some alone time where they talked about the last time Tonya was home before she left for college. They discussed how they really enjoyed sharing their first sexual experience together. How they wish they had more time to enjoy it then, before her parents came home. But that just made it more memorable.

That weekend the group played games, watched movies, ate junk food, laughed, talked about their past, present and futures. Tonya told them about school, how she missed home, her room mate was a smart, party girl and how she was planning for the next year to be very hard and busy with school. John didn't really have much to say. He was still working at the shoe store at the mall. He didn't like it at first but now he was getting the hang of it. Mike talked about his room mate, his girlfriend and how he decided to major in business with a minor in art.

"Art, where did that idea come from?" asked John.

"That's something no one knew about me, I've always liked art, could even draw a little, but it was never good enough for anyone to see", replied Mike.

"Well I'm glad you decided on something but we would like to see your drawings one day", said James.

"Maybe when I get a little better. What have you been up to James?" asked Mike.

"Nothing much, you know working at the Chocolate Palace, about to become the next assistant manager and learning to drive", answered James.

"That's not nothing, that's great news, a promotion and you haven't even been there a year yet, congrats man", said Mike.

"Yea, congratualations", Tonya and John said at the same time.

"Yea, I guess, who would have

known I would be good at making chocolate. The only thing I get out of it is a raise. I feel like I've been doing the manager's job since November", James said. "But I have been looking forward to taking my drivers test sometime in the next two weeks".

"That good, you'll finally be able to drive "the bird". Don't get mad if I ask you for a ride every now and again", replied John.

"Just as long as you're giving up gas money. So do any of you plan on getting a drivers license?" asked James.

"You know I can't afford a car, so I'll just use you and the bus for now", replied John.

"Maybe one day when I have a real job instead of work study at school or maybe I'll just wait for someone to buy me one", Mike added as he pushed James's shoulder.

"Well maybe if you were as smart as James someone would have", Tonya commented, "but I don't know about driving cause it too many crazies on the street".

"That's what I thought at first", said James.

"Look at her taking up for her man, I was just joking", Mike interrupted.

"We know, but that's what you do for love. As I was saying", James continued, "you just got to focus on the way you drive and just be on the look out for those crazy drivers. If you worry too much about the other drivers it will mess up your driving".

"See that's what I've been missing, James is always telling us how it is. Its been that way since the first time I met him", said John. "I remember his first words to me were, don't think I'm being rude, I've just been through a lot in my life".

"Aww man I thought I was the only one you said that to", said Mike, "but it really was no reason for those words, cause after a couple of week we were all the best of friends".

"I only said that because it was true. I didn't know that I would get as close to y'all so fast or that you two would become the brothers I never had", replied James.

"See we have to do this more often. I know I haven't been with the group as long as you three have, but I see you young men as my second family", said Tonya.

"I think we all feel the same way. We must always keep in touch. Now let's go to bed, I don't want us to be sleepy on our last day with James", said John.

Little did the group know that was the last time they would spend together for a while. Tonya and Mike was busy with school; John was busy working, while trying to save whatever he could and James was busy being assistant manager, trying to figure out his life and spending as much time with Tonya as he could. It was easier now that he was driving. Sometimes James would sneak into Tonya's dorm room for booty calls when her room mate was away.

Somehow James still found time to talk to his grandfather about the important stuff.

"So grandpa how long were you and grandma together before you proposed?" James asked.

"Oh wow, you know I'm getting old, but I think it was about four or five years, why are planning something", answered Mr. Harrison.

"You know I'm always making plans but there's a couple of things I have to do before I get to that point, I was just wondering", replied James.

"Well keep me informed and let me know if you need any help or advice", said Mr. Harrison.

"Will do pops will do", said James as he walked out the room.

Within the next couple of weeks if James wasn't at work or with Tonya, he was on his computer looking for apartments. He was so serious about finding a good one, he started looking into his trust fund. His grandparents told him they started it with $15,000 and added to it every month since he moved with them. After doing some math and research James figured that he had a decent amount of money but he didn't want to use it all at once. James figured he would use some to get an apartment and it might be enough to help buy a house for Tonya and himself later.

But he knew he needed to live on his own first. Two months after he turned nineteen James sat his grandparents down to have a little talk.

"Grandmom, granddad, I would like to thank you for all you have done for me and all you've taught me", started James. "But I believe it is time for me to live on my own and really get my life together".

"But your only nineteen, you have so much time. What's the rush?" asked Nancy.

"No rush, I just don't think I can fully decide what I want to do with my life until I live on my own", James continued.

"I thought working was you being

on your own. For once I have to agree with Nancy. You've only been out of high school for a year. Are you sure this is what you want to do?" asked Mike.

"Yes, I know it seems kind of soon but in that year I've learned a lot about myself and where I want to be in five years", James replied. "But in order for me to get there I have to be on my own, without you guys as my safety net. Learning from you guys how to pay bills and now paying my car insurance made me think I could live on my own".

"Well we're not going to make a big deal about your desicion. You know how we feel and you know will always be here for you" said Mike.

"That's all I can ask for. Now with that being said I've already found me a place and I'm moving out in two weeks", said James. "I will need one of you to be a co-signer for my lease though.

"Hey now don't be treating us like no job with your two week notice", said Nancy with a smirk on her face.

"I hadn't planned on it being so soon but I caught a break on a two year lease rental apartment by Tonya's college", replied James, "its only $550 a month and it comes with a stove and refrigerator.

"How did you get a deal like that? So does this mean Tonya will be moving in with you?" asked Nancy.

"The place needs a little work so

the landlord went down on the rent", answered James.

"What kind of work, do you need any help?" asked Mike.

"Mostly paint, little cracks here and there and I think he said the carpet needed to be cleaned, but yea granddad you can help if you want", replied James. "Tonya and I have talked about her moving in but not right away. She still have some school stuff to do and I don't want to interfere with that".

"That's good, when can we see the apartment?" asked Nancy.

"I'm going to drop off the down payment in a couple of days, I'll let you know depending on what kind of shape it's in", said James.

"So just to be clear mister, what are your plans for the next five years?" asked Nancy.

"I plan to live by myself for about a year at the apartment. Then when the time is right and Tonya is almosted finished with her clinical training, I will ask her to move in with me. If that goes well after six months I plan to ask her to marry me. If she says yes then some where down the line we will buy a house and maybe start a family", said James. "Oh and grandma I'm gonna need you to help me pick out some little things for the apartment, cause you always know how to bargain shop".

"Ok then, just let me know what you're looking for and I'll tell you where to find it", said Nancy as she went to start dinner with a tear in her eyes.

"You know you're wrong, right", said Mike.

"For what?" asked James, "She asked me what my plans were and I told her".

"That's not what I meant. You asked her to help you shop and then complemented her so she wouldn't have anything to say about your well thought out plans of you getting engaged", replied Mike. "Very sneaky but very smart".

"Well all these years I've learned a few things but I really didn't know it was going to work like that", said James.

Chapter 8
Planning The Future

Two weeks had passed, Mike helped James fix up his apartment. Nancy helped James pick out a couch, some pictures and some other little things. Within a week it was starting to look like a home to James, but in the back of his mind he was a little scared of being alone. He enjoyed the apartment more when Tonya came to visited. Now they didn't have sneak around anymore to have sex. She really liked the apartment or maybe it was just that anything was better compared to a dorm room. James and Tonya tried not to but they were already making plans for when Tonya moved in. James later received a phone call from John. John apologized for not being there to help James move into his new place. James told him not to worry about it. Besides he didn't have too much stuff to move anyway. James gave John an open invition to visit as long as he called first.

"So how's the family, how are the little rug rats doing?" asked James.

"They're good, everyones good. Little J is graduating from middle school in June and my grown little sister is the smartest fifth grader I know", answered John.

"They grew up so quick, but I'm sure that's what our parents said about us. Speaking of growing up I got to finish getting my place together, talk to you later", said James.

"Alright man congrats again, talk to you soon", said John as they hung up the phones.

While James finished fixing up his apartment and organizing his bills, he thought about his future. He knew that it wouldn't be easy working hard to pay his bills and trying to spend so much time with Tonya. But he knew once he hired more crew members at work, he would have more time for everything.

As weeks turned to months James became more and more comfortable being on his own. He set up a schedule to make sure he paid his bills on time and balanced his money so he could buy groceries and get gas. James even opened up his first checking account, something his granddad had been telling him to do since graduation. The times James was home from work he didn't watch tv or play any games. At first, he just sat with his thoughts, thinking about his future. As he thought about what he wanted to do, most things required schooling. He knew since he was on his own now school was not an option. The one thing that kept popping in his head was writing. He wasn't sure exactly what he wanted to write at first. He started with poems; then he thought about writing children books. James remembered that was something him and his mother talked about when he was little. He knew because of his schedule it would take some time. So he started carrying around a notebook everywhere he went to write down ideas.

Mr. & Mrs. Harrison came to visit as often as they could until they knew he was ok living by himself. Then they just called to check in. John stopped by once or twice. They spent time catching up, playing video games and making prank calls to Mike at school. After the first few months Tonya was spending the night a least once a week. They called it a trial period before she moved in, but it was really that James didn't want her to leave. As much as James knew he needed to live by himself, it was just something about Tonya's presence that made him always want her around. Whatever free time they had they would always try to spend it together, either going out somewhere or staying at the apartment cuddled up watching tv. When the time came for Tonya to actually move in, James was in heaven. He got to wake up to her everyday and go to sleep next to her most nights depending on their schedules. They had fun living together, eating breakfast in the morning and James having dinner ready when Tonya came home. Tonya and James got to know each other a little better everyday. From their habits to their likes and dislikes about different situations. James learned that Tonya was an early morning person even on the days she didn't have anywhere to go. Tonya learned that James liked to sleep in, something she had to break him out of. They played games and watched tv together on their days off. They talked a lot about their future. How they didn't want to renew the lease to the apartment but instead buy a house together, if they got their finances in order in time. They talked about how since neither of them had a big family they didn't need to have a big wedding. Tonya and James also agreed that they were undecided on having children. They both thought it would be nice to have them but not right away. They wanted Tonya's career to come first. James joked about him being a house husband after the baby was born. James even told Tonya his ideas about writing children books.

"As many books that you've read in your life, you'd be really great at writing one", said Tonya.

"Yea, I read somewhere that reading books is the first steps to writing them. Now all I need is the time", replied James.

"Finding time is the easiest part. I'm pretty sure you already have a book or two written in your note pad over there", Tonya said as she pointed across the room.

"You know you're probably right. It's almost time for another one", said James. "I'm sure I'll find time sooner or later, cause I don't think I'm going to be working for Mr. Stevenson to much longer".

"Why not, what's wrong?" asked

Tonya.

"I know I haven't been working there that long but it feels like I have", answered James. "They're always coming up with new rules and now that I'm assistant manager nothing has changed. I still feel like I'm doing everyone's job with no help".

"Well I know its hard and you've been going through this since the beginning but don't do nothing crazy. We're on our own now", replied Tonya, "and I'm not going back to my parents".

"I know babe. You know I would never make us broke", said James, "but you'll take care of me right".

"Yea, just wait until I get licenses

and hired in somewhere, before you make any changes", Tonya said.

"Will do dear, will do", said James.

After about three months of Tonya and James living together James started going ring shopping. The first time was with Tonya just to see what type of jewelry she liked. Then later he went with his grandmother, to have a woman's point of view on the best engagement ring ever.

"So when's the big day? When do you plan to pop the question?" asked Nancy.

"I was planning on doing it for our five year anniversary, but I don't know. She might expect something like that and I want it to be a total surprise", answered James.

"So what do you plan on doing with the rest of your trust fund money?" asked Nancy.

"I plan to use it to buy a house" answered James.

"I need this in a size five and do you think you can have it ready in two weeks?" James asked the clerk at the jewelry store.

The clerk nodded as he gave James his receipt.

"So, how are you and granddad doing without me in the house?" asked James as they walked out of the store.

"We're fine, the house is quiet, it's

almost like it was before you moved in", answered Nancy. "The only difference is that we got use to you being in the house. There's no need to ask how you and Tonya are, seeing that we're ring shopping months a head of your plan".

"Yea it's great, much better than we both thought possible", James said. "I was a little scared at first".

"I am glad you two are happy, but what were you scared of. It couldn't have been the money. You already had that planned before you moved", inquired Nancy.

"No, the money wasn't what I was scared of. Living by myself is one thing but I didn't wanna move to fast and mess things up with Tonya", replied James. "Look at the time, thanks for all your help grandma. I gotta get home and fiqure out what's for dinner. Tell granddad I said hi".

"You're welcome dear, whatever I can do to help, you know I'm here for you", said Nancy, "and I'm sure you two will be ok. Tonya will still love you and whatever crazy habits you may have.

James went home to start dinner before Tonya came home, but before he got started he took a seat in his thinking chair. This was the chair he brought from home. He used it everytime he needed to figure out something. This time he needed to think of the best way to propose to Tonya. But he thought for so long, he looked up and Tonya was walking though the door.

"Sorry, I didn't make anything for dinner tonight I got caught up thinking about stuff", said James.

"That's ok I brought food home. You said you was out with your grandmother and I know how y'all get. I'm surprised you're home already", said Tonya.

"Yea I just got home bout a half an hour ago", replied James, "so how was your day?"

"It was ok. You know same oh same oh. Just getting us ready for the test in a couple of months. I think I'm mostly ready, I just have to work on taking blood presure", said Tonya.

"I believe in you, you'll be ready when the time comes", replied

James, "what's for dinner?"

"Just burgers and fries", said Tonya, "so what were you thinking about so hard?"

"Just our future. I was just putting everything together", James replied not wanting to tell her the whole truth. "What would you think if we got a two bedroom house. That way I could have my own room to write in?"

"I think that's a great idea, as long as the taxes aren't high, there's a shower and not too much work has to be done on it", answered Tonya.

"Ok, I'll keep all that in mind when I go online", said James, "I agree with you on everything, especially the not a lot of work part. After what

I had to do with this apartment, I don't wanna go through that again. We just have to make sure we have all the money saved before hand".

"With us working so much we don't have time to spend any money, so I'm not worried about that. I am worried that if we don't eat this food it's going be cold", said Tonya, "you know you don't own a microwave".

"Ha ha very funny, I have a stove. I'll make sure we have a microwave at our house ma'am", James said as they walked into the kitchen. "You know all this talk about the future, I had a great blast from the past two days ago. You will never guess who I hired last week".

"Who?" asked Tonya.

"My old friend Danny. I didn't know who he was at first cause he's grown up and has a different last name", answered James.

"That's great, did he know who you were?" asked Tonya.

"Not right away, but he came to work and asked me what my last name was. We put two and two together and figured it out. Every chance we got at work we were catching each other up on our lives", replied James.

"I'm so happy for you. When do I get to meet Danny?" asked Tonya.

"I'll have to see when he's free. I think you are really going to like him", said James.

Within the next couple of days all James could talk about was Danny did this and Danny said that. By the time Tonya met Danny she felt like she had known him as long as James had.

"So Danny, I've heard some stories about you and James at the orphanage", said Tonya.

"Well you must've heard that I was the one that got blamed for all the trouble James and I got into. Everyone loved James, he could do no wrong", replied Danny.

"James I know you didn't let poor little Danny take the blame for everything?" asked Tonya.

"No, but that was the crazy part. They could catch both of us, but always said that Danny was a bad influence on me and he would get in trouble", replied James.

"I think they just felt sorry for him cause all he had been through. They felt the same even after James was there for over a year", Danny added.

"Anything you can tell me that I may not know about James?" asked Tonya.

"James always use to be the first to talk about people", answered Danny.

"That's funny cause he use to talk about one of our friends everytime he made fun of people", said Tonya.

"Well I was only eight or nine years old. It's different compared to Mike being fifteen, sixteen. It was funnier back then", replied James.

"Well, I would love to hear more stories about those times one day because James doesn't talk about the orphanage much. I have to go get ready for work tomorrow. It was very nice meeting you Danny, sorry I can't stay longer", said Tonya.

"Nice meeting you too Tonya. Believe me I have a lot of stories to tell. We can swap stories one day", replied Danny.

"Hey now no one will be telling any stories that I don't want told", said James.

Danny and James spent a little more time catching up before saying their goodbyes.

"So what was your adoptive parents like?" asked Danny.

"Oh my goodness, I can't believe I haven't told you yet", replied James, "first off they were\are great. The best part is they turned out to be my grandparents".

"What? Are you serious, from your mother or father?" asked Danny.

"From my father", answered James.

"That's crazy, that must have been great, how did you find out?" asked Danny.

"Long story short, I saw some photos of their son, compared them to the pictures I had of my parents and then we took a DNA test", replied James. "What about your parents? "

"Well they're great. My mom is a great cook, she even had a catering company and my dad was a lawyer, replied Danny, "I think he still practice every so often".

"I'm probably the last person that should be asking this, but are you planning on going to college, if so what for?" asked James.

"Yeah I plan to. I plan to follow in my dad's foot steps and become a lawyer", answered Danny.

"Wow that's great. When do you plan to go to college?" asked James.

"Maybe in about two years. My dad told me how long and hard it would be, so I thought I would take sometime, save some money before I go", replied Danny. "Plus my parents said they would match whatever I save".

"Well that's great. How are you liking the Chocolate Palace?" asked James.

"Oh its great. Unlike those other kids in there, I'm use to working. I've been going to work with my father since I was sixteen. Speaking of, I have to go to work tomorrow boss, but we must do this again. We still have a lot of time to make up".

"I know it's been a lifetime right, see you tomorrow", said James.

"Alright man see you", said Danny as he walked out the door.

Chapter 9
The Proposal

The year 2005 had came and it was a big year for James. He was turning 21, buying a house and planned to propose to Tonya. Now he just had to finding the right house and figure out how he would propose. Unfortunately, James had to work on his birthday, so Tonya made him dinner when he got home. Steak, potatoes, broccoli with some champagne and everyone called leaving messages on his phone. Every chance James got free he was either looking for houses or thinking about how to ask Tonya to marry him. He wanted everything to be a surprise and special, which is why his mother had the ring. It wasn't that he thought Tonya would find it but the apartment didn't have too many places to hide it. Within the next couple of months James had found the perfect house for Tonya and himself. Tonya fell in love with it almost as soon as she saw it. It was everything they were looking for. Three bedrooms, one bathroom with shower, big living room, average size dinning room, kitchen, basement and attic. The best part was the property taxes would only be about one hundred and fifty dollars a month. James and Tonya put their money together to put up the down payment with plans to pay off the rest with James's trust fund money. Once everything was paid in full they took time off work and rented a moving van. They were on their way to moving into their new home and starting their new life together.

After buying the house they set everything up; the couch from the apartment went in front of the window in the living room across from the tv, Tonya brought a table, where they put all their plaque and awards on. James's thinking chair went in his writing room with his computer. Lucky for them Tonya's parents gave them a dinning room set and they were able to take the stove and refigrator from the apartment so they didn't have to buy those. After getting their bills together, buying extra chairs, a new bed and other little things they needed, they still had some money saved. With Tonya having a guarantee, working full time at the hosiptal in a month or two, James planned to started working part time within six months. That would give him time to start working on his book.

They had to plan their house warming party around Tonya's busy schedule. Luckily she had a couple of days off before she took the test for her RN licenses. Most of them she used to study and prepare for her test but she took one day to have the house warming. Everyone was there, her parents; James's grandparents; friends from both their jobs; John and Mike even took time out to come and everyone got a chance to meet Danny. Everyone was there enjoying themselves, James had a great idea. He asked everyone to gather in the living room and poured them some champagne.

"I would like to thank everyone for coming out today to celebrate this moment with Tonya and I", James said as he pulled Tonya close to him, "we've been together for almost six years now but this last year with us living together has been the best year of my life".

"I really love living with you too babe", Tonya added with a big smile on her face, "if I didn't I guess I'm stuck with you now".

"Yep, but for real, Tonya is one of the brightest people I know. She completes me. She's my happiness. Did y'all know that she will be a licensed doctor by next week",

James said to make Tonya blush and turn away from him.

At this time he got on one knee and took out the ring, a 1\5 round diamond center stone with additional round accent diamonds lining the sterling silver band.

"I'm not only looking forward to enjoying this wonderful house with her but spending the rest of my life with her, if she'd have me" James said, "Tonya will you do me the honors of becoming my wife".

Tonya turned around before she realized what he'd said.

"Tonya will you marry me?", James asked again.

After a long silence Tonya took

James hands, said yes. The whole room lit up with excitement.

After congratulating the couple and admiring the ring, everyone got a tour of the house. Then went back to enjoying the party. Later that night John and Mike pulled James to the side.

"So since you have Danny back in your life, which one of us is going to be your best man?" asked Mike.

"Let me see, which one of you gave me the best gift today", James replied, "just kidding. I'm not going to have a big traditional wedding so I'm not going to need a best man but you'll all be invited. Mike you're not getting jealous of Danny are you, there's enough of me to go around".

"So have you picked a date yet?" asked John.

"Well I have a date in mind but I have to get the ok from Tonya", replied James, "speaking of Tonya let me go see where she's at.

When he found Tonya she was in a corner with Danny looking at the ring.

"What's wrong", James asked, "you don't like the ring?"

"No, I love it. I was just telling Danny how I just can't believe everything was so real. I never would've imagined in my wildest dreams that any of this would happen so soon", Tonya said as tears of joy rolled down her face, "I thought the house and me getting my

RN licenses was big for one year but now I'm engaged, wow".

"Seeing you happy makes me happy and maybe when you're less overwhelmed we can talk more about the wedding", James said, "if you want you can go lay down and I'll see all the guest out, love you".

"Ok, love you too", said Tonya as she walked to the bed room.

After thanking everyone once again for coming as they left, James thanked his grandparents for coming before he went to check on Tonya.

"Remember no babies before marriage", Nancy whispered to James.

"Tonya's on birth control but

thanks for the advice, love you", James whispered back.

The next morning Tonya was up cooking breakfast and apologizing for being so emotional the night before.

"I don't know what came over me. It was just the thought of me actually owning a house with the man I love, the proposal and then this beautiful ring", Tonya said as she started to tear up again, "it was all a little much I guess".

"As much as I love to see you happy, I hate to see you cry even happy tears, so no more surprises for a while", said James. "After I get off work and when you get done with your test, we can sit down and make our future plans together".

"Ok, that'll work. Go ahead eat up, I didn't make this for my health. I got to go get ready, see you later, love you", Tonya said as she gave James a kiss and walked out the kicten, "and you know I'm going to be a nurse right".

"Yes, doctor just sounded better last night", replied James, "I love you too".

So when they both got home later that day, they sat down and talked.

"Before we start I just want to say I love you, but I don't know if I can promise you I will be the best husband because I don't know how. I will promise to be the best me I can be", James started.

"Well that's all I can ask for, I promise to do the same", said Tonya.

"Well you know I'm always planning, so if you have any questions or concerns stop me at anytime", James added. "I was thinking in two years I would quit my job to focus more on my book\books. I would like to get married next year on our anniversary. Nothing big just family and a few friends, maybe an outside wedding if you want. Does everything sound ok so far".

"Yes, I'm listening, go ahead", replied Tonya.

"Ok, then after about a year or two of us being married depending on how my book sells and how you are in your career, I thought we could have another talk about growing our family", James continued.

"Well I agree with you on almost everything, but we're still young so I would change the having babies part to four or five years after marriage. Just in case I wanted to go back to school to get my bachelors degree", said Tonya. "Oh and not doubting your talent, but what is your plan if your book or books don't do well".

"Ok, I think I can wait the five years. And if I can't sell my book to the satisfaction that you and I agree upon, then I will find me another nine to five and we will live our life in love as husband and wife", James replied.

Made in the USA
Charleston, SC
21 February 2017